Energy Matters

Alan Fraser · Illustrated by Bryan Miller

M000007508

Contents

Rigby®

A Harcourt Achieve Imprint

www.Rigby.com
1-800-531-5015

Henry's Idea

On the second day of summer vacation, Henry decided that it was going to be the best summer ever. He was finally old enough to go to science camp. He could spend all day doing experiments and learning amazing new things.

He also would get the entire house all to himself for one hour every day! His camp ended one hour before his parents would get off of work. He had a whole hour alone to do whatever he wanted. He could read, play video games, or play the radio as loud as he wanted! Of course, there were rules.

The Rules

1. Never open the front door to strangers.

2. Always clean up after yourself.

3. Never use the stove or light any fires.

Henry was having a great summer, but something started to worry him. He noticed that his parents looked very tired when they came home from work every day. He tried to think of something he could do to help.

One day he had a great idea—he would have dinner ready when his parents got home! He decided to make sandwiches. He made an entire plateful of all different kinds of sandwiches, even peanut butter and banana sandwiches for dessert! He could hardly wait until his parents got home.

"Sit down and relax!" he said when they walked through the door.

"That's sweet, Henry," his dad said, "but we need to get dinner started."

"It's already finished!" Henry said with a huge grin on his face.

His parents were so happy when they saw the sandwiches that Henry decided to make dinner every night.

Henry was glad that he could help. But there was one problem—he was getting sick of sandwiches.

Sandwiches were OK now and then, but it had been a whole week since they had eaten a hot dinner. Henry didn't want to stop helping, but he didn't know how many more sandwiches he could eat.

He wished he could make burgers and fries for dinner. He would have to use the stove, though, and that was definitely against the rules.

"Mom, wouldn't it be great if I could use the stove?" Henry asked at dinner. "Then I could really have a great meal waiting for you and Dad!"

Henry's mom and dad looked shocked.

"Henry, don't even think about it!" his mother said.

"Henry, you know the rules!" added his father.

Henry just looked down at his plate. There had to be a way that he could follow the rules *and* make something besides sandwiches.

The next day, Henry learned the most amazing thing at science camp. He decided to try it at home.

When Henry's mom and dad got home from work they smelled something wonderful in the air.

"Our neighbors must be having a barbeque," Henry's dad said.

Henry waved at his parents as they walked up to the house.

"Hi, Mom! Hi, Dad!" Henry said with a smile. "Come and see what I've made for dinner!"

"I'll bet I can guess," said his mom.

"It's not sandwiches!" Henry said.

"Oh," said his dad, sounding more interested.

They followed Henry into the kitchen.

"Look!" Henry said.

He had set the table for dinner. There were plates and napkins and glasses. A big pitcher of ice water was ready for pouring. Next to that were bottles of mustard and ketchup.

"Did you cook hamburgers for dinner, Henry?" his dad asked.

His mom put her hands on her hips.

"Henry Jones!" she said. "I cannot believe you broke Rule 3!"

"But Mom, I didn't!" Henry said.

"Are you sure?" she asked, still frowning.

"Of course I'm sure!" Henry said. "Come outside. You'll see."

Henry's dad looked confused. "Well, if you didn't use the stove, how did you cook dinner?" he asked.

"I didn't do anything wrong, I promise!" he said, laughing. "Today at camp we learned how to make a solar cooker. I used mine to cook hot dogs for dinner."

At first it just looked like a shoebox lined with aluminum foil. But Henry showed them how he had used a wire coat hanger to hold the hot dogs in place. He explained how the sun had cooked the hot dogs.

"See? It's completely safe!" he said.

"Wow," said his mom, "I guess you're learning a lot at science camp!"

Henry could tell that his parents were proud. He was proud, too.

"Come on," Henry said, "our dinner is probably getting cold."

His parents followed him inside.

Henry smiled happily as they ate dinner. He still had three more weeks of science camp left. Who knew what other great things he would learn?

"Hey," he said, "I've been thinking. I have a good idea for a dessert that I can make when winter comes. You both like snow cones, right?"

What Is Energy?

Energy All Around

You have probably heard someone say, "I don't have any energy today!" Or maybe someone has told you, "I can't believe how much energy you have!"

But how do you get energy? You can't buy it at the mall or find it in a store. Energy isn't something you can touch or see, but it's all around you. Anytime something moves or changes, energy is there.

This athlete needs energy to run.

Even tiny flowers use energy to grow.

We cannot live, move, work, or even sleep without energy. We need energy to keep us warm, to breathe, to grow, and to think. Kittens need energy to purr. Flowers need energy to grow. Even trains, boats, and motorcycles need energy to move! Almost everything you can think of uses energy.

Different Kinds of Energy

Energy is everywhere, but not all energy is the same. There are three kinds of energy: electrical, chemical, and nuclear.

Every time we turn on a switch, we use electrical energy. It can give us light and heat and can make radios or televisions turn on.

electrical energy

Chemical energy can be found right inside your body! When you eat, your body uses the food to make energy. Gasoline for cars is another kind of chemical energy.

Nuclear energy is much less common. It is made from tiny bits of matter called atoms. Scientists can split atoms up or join them together to create huge amounts of energy.

chemical energy

nuclear energy

If you want to see where most energy comes from, look up at the sky. The sun is a huge energy source!

When plants grow, they take in sunlight and store it. Actually, all of your energy comes from the sun. Think about it; you get your energy from food. Since all our foods come either from plants or from animals that eat plants, all of our energy comes from the sun!

The sun's energy is also stored in **fossil fuels** such as coal, oil, and natural gas. Fossil fuels are remains of living things from millions of years ago, which used the sun's energy when they were alive.

We use the sun's energy every day!

Energy for Machines

Most of the machines in our homes and factories use electricity from a **power plant**. Small objects like flashlights, radios, and cell phones use electricity stored in batteries.

Large, moving machines such as cars, airplanes, and some trains, get energy by burning fuels made from oil.

Airplane engines get energy from oil.

Non-Renewable Supplies of Energy

About 85 percent of the energy we use today comes from coal, oil, or natural gas. These things are used to make both electrical and chemical energy. Fossil fuels took many millions of years to form deep under the earth's surface. Once they are used up, we cannot make any more. That is why coal, oil, and natural gas are **non-renewable** forms of energy.

Fossil Fuels

	Amount Available	Amount Used Each Year	How Long Before It Runs Out
Coal	1,200 billion tons	2.2 billion tons	550 years
Oil	140 billion tons	3.2 billion tons	45 years
Natural Gas	120 billion tons	1.9 billion tons	60 years

Companies drill deep into the earth to get oil.

But scientists are finding sources of energy that will not run out and will not hurt the earth.

The sun's energy can be collected and turned into solar energy. Modern wind turbines produce electricity using the energy of the wind. Hydroelectric power plants use the energy of running or falling water to produce electricity. In Iceland, scientists use the heat of the earth to create geothermal energy.

Scientists have even found a way that garbage can be burned and turned into energy!

Solar panels gather the sun's rays and turn them into energy.

Renewable Energy Sources

Energy Source	Where Available	Advantages	Disadvantages
wind	high or windy places	• safe • no harmful gases • low cost	• only works when wind is blowing • takes a lot of space
sun	sunny areas	• safe • no harmful gases	• only works when sun is shining • high cost
hydroelectric	fast-flowing rivers	• safe • no harmful gases	• takes a lot of space • high cost • can hurt fish
geothermal	only where hot rocks come near the earth's surface	• safe • no harmful gases • low cost • works all of the time	• takes a lot of space

These **renewable** energy sources can give energy without hurting the earth or people. And unlike fossil fuels, they will never run out. But some of these new ways of producing energy can still be noisy, costly, or take up a lot of space.

No one has found a perfect source of energy, but scientists are trying new things every day!

Glossary

fossil fuels coal, oil, and natural gas

non-renewable describes something that cannot be replaced

power plant a place where fuel is turned into electricity

renewable describes something that can be replaced